D0934539

Community Helpers

# Garbage Collectors

by Rebecca Pettiford

Bullfrog Books

# Ideas for Parents and Teachers

Bullfrog Books let children practice reading informational text at the earliest reading levels. Repetition, familiar words, and photo labels support early readers.

## Before Reading

• Discuss the cover photo. Who might this book be about?

• Look at the picture glossary together. Read and discuss the words.

## Read the Book

• "Walk" through the book and look at the photos. Let the child ask questions. Point out the photo labels.

• Read the book to the child, or have him or her read independently.

## After Reading

• Prompt the child to think more. Ask: Does a garbage collector come to your house? Have you seen garbage collectors in other places?

Bullfrog Books are published by Jump!
5357 Penn Avenue South
Minneapolis, MN 55419
www.jumplibrary.com

Library of Congress Cataloging-in-Publication Data

Pettiford, Rebecca.
  Garbage collectors / by Rebecca Pettiford.
    pages cm. — (Community helpers)
  Includes index.)
  Summary: "This photo-illustrated book for early readers describes the work garbage collectors do in our communities. Includes a picture glossary"— Provided by publisher.
  ISBN 978-1-62031-157-8 (hardcover) —
  ISBN 978-1-62496-244-8 (ebook)
  1. Sanitation workers—Juvenile literature.
  2. Refuse and refuse disposal—Juvenile literature.
  I. Title.
  HD8039.S257P48 2015
  363.72023—dc23
                                          2014032097

Series Editor: Wendy Dieker
Series Designer: Ellen Huber
Book Designer: Anna Peterson
Photo Researcher: Anna Peterson

Photo Credits: All photos from Shutterstock except: Alamy, 12–13; Corbis, 5, 8–9, 20; Dreamstime, 22; Getty, cover; iStock, 6–7; Superstock, 24; Thinkstock, 12–13, 16–17, 17, 23tl, 23tr, 23br.

Printed in the United States of America at Corporate Graphics in North Mankato, Minnesota.

# Table of Contents

# Picking Up the Trash

Bo wants to be a garbage collector.

**What do they do?**

They pick up garbage.
They take it away.

Look! It's a garbage truck.

Ed drives.

**Jay rides on the back.**

Stan is at a house.

He gets off the truck.

He gets the bin.

He dumps it.

**bin**

We recycle. We use a special bin.
We put paper in it.

Dan and Bob pick it up.

They empty it.

Al works in a city.

He loads a dumpster.

Wow! It is big.

dumpster

15

It is fall.

Mel picks up bags.

What's inside?

Leaves.

Jose is at the dump.

He empties the truck.

# Garbage collectors do good work!

# On the Garbage Truck

**hopper**
The part of a garbage truck where the trash is carried on the way to the dump.

**cab**
The part of the truck where the driver sits and drives the truck.

**lift**
A machine on the truck that can carry the bin up to dump it into the truck.

# Picture Glossary

**bin**
Container for garbage.

**dumpster**
A large garbage bin that can be lifted onto a garbage truck.

**dump**
A place to put the garbage; also called a landfill.

**recycle bin**
A bin that holds items that can be recycled or reused such as paper, glass, and plastic.

# Index

# To Learn More

Learning more is as easy as 1, 2, 3.

1) Go to www.factsurfer.com

2) Enter "garbage collectors" into the search box.

3) Click the "Surf" button to see a list of websites.

With factsurfer.com, finding more information is just a click away.